The Rockwool Foundation Research Unit

Losing the stigma of incarceration:
Does serving a sentence with electronic monitoring causally improve post-release labor market outcomes?

Lars Højsgaard Andersen & Signe Hald Andersen

University Press of Southern Denmark
Odense 2012

Losing the stigma of incarceration: Does serving a sentence with electronic monitoring causally improve post-release labor market outcomes?

Study Paper No. 40

Published by:
© The Rockwool Foundation Research Unit and
University Press of Southern Denmark

Copying from this book is permitted only within
institutions that have agreements with CopyDan,
and only in accordance with the limitations laid
down in the agreement

Address:
The Rockwool Foundation Research Unit
Sølvgade 10, 2.tv
DK-1307 Copenhagen K

Telephone   +45 33 34 48 00

Fax   +45 33 34 48 99

E-mail   forskningsenheden@rff.dk

Home page   www.rff.dk

ISBN 978-87-90199-67-8
ISSN 0908-3979
January 2012
Print run: 350
Printed by   Specialtrykkeriet Viborg A/S

Price: 60.00 DKK, including 25% VAT

Contents

Abstract 5

Introduction 6

Why should we expect non-custodial sentences to matter? 7

    Stigmatization 7

    Loss of capital 8

    Negative effects of EM? 9

Electronic monitoring in Denmark 9

    Identification strategy 10

    Method 11

Data and variables 13

    Variables 15

Results 18

    Results from DiD and DiD matching analyses 19

Sensitivity analysis 20

Discussion and conclusion 24

Appendix 26

References 30

Losing the stigma of incarceration: Does serving a sentence with electronic monitoring causally improve post-release labor market outcomes?

Lars Højsgaard Andersen & Signe Hald Andersen

Abstract

Many Western countries now use electronic monitoring (EM) of some offenders as an alternative to more traditional forms of punishments such as imprisonment. While the main reason for introducing EM is the growing prison population, politicians and administrators also believe that this type of punishment achieves a positive effect by reducing recidivism and the probability of post-release marginalization. The small existing empirical literature on the effect of EM finds mixed support for this belief, but is, however, based on very small sample sizes. We expand this literature by studying the causal effect of EM on social benefit dependency after the sentence has been served. We use administrative data from Statistics Denmark that include information on all Danish offenders who have served their sentence under EM rather than in prison. We compare post-release dependency rates for this group with outcomes for a historical control group of convicted offenders who would have served their sentences with EM had the option been available – i.e. who are identical to the EM group on all observed and unobserved characteristics. We find that serving a sentence with EM significantly decreases the dependency rates after release.

Introduction

During the last 40 years, the US has witnessed a striking increase in prison populations. Between 1980 and 2000 the number of incarcerated Americans grew from 500,000 to 2,000,000 individuals, and the number continues to rise (Justice Policy Institute Report, 2000). The increase in the US is unparalleled by that in any other country; however, we also see tougher strategies towards criminals in several other countries. In Denmark, the penal law has been amended 62 times during the last 20 years, and most of these changes have represented increased strictness involving more severe punishments and longer prison sentences. As a result, Denmark now suffers from prison overcrowding, and in 2008 was reported to have its highest number of prison inmates in 60 years (Lehmann, 2008). Significantly, in neither the US nor Denmark does the rising prison population result from an increase in the crime rate or an upsurge in serious crime. Rather, the changed and toughened strategies are mainly the consequence of the increased use of "tough-on-crime"-policies (Raphael & Stoll, 2009).

The observed increase in prison populations has obvious financial consequences. Not only is it costly to keep people in jail, but imprisoned citizens also contribute less to society, as incarceration prevents them from participating at the ordinary labor market. However, apart from these obvious consequences that can easily be identified, we have very little knowledge of the effects of imprisonment (Killias & Villetaz, 2008; Bushway & Paternoster, 2009). In theory, imprisonment may on the one hand facilitate rehabilitation, but on the other hand cause stigmatization, deterioration in human capital and increased identification with the criminal world. The first process – that of rehabilitation – should improve offenders' chances of succeeding at the labor market in particular and in society in general, once the sentence has been served. But the second process that brings about stigmatization, deterioration in human capital, etc., will worsen the outcomes of the ex-prisoner, and bring unemployment, poor social relations and continued criminal activity. Whether the one or the other process dominates will make a huge difference, not only to the ex-prisoner himself or herself, but also to the rest of the society. In particular, if prison sentences in general, and longer prison sentences in particular, decrease desistance rates, the rise in prison populations will lead to even more crime in the future.

In sum, we suggest that understanding the effects of imprisonment is important, both in general, but also particularly at a time when we are witnessing an increasing prison population. For this purpose, we need to answer the counterfactual question of what would have happened to the offenders sent to prison if they had not been imprisoned. That is the purpose of our study.

Answering this question is, however, no trivial task, as we never observe the same offender in both states – with and without serving the prison term. A few existing studies resolve this problem by using data from experiments that randomize custodial and non-custodial sentences, mainly community service (see, for example, Killias et al., 2010, for a review of the literature; and see Villetaz et al., 2006; Killias & Villetaz, 2008; Renzema & May-Wilson, 2005). This is a strong design that exploits the differences in the two sentence types but similarities in the two groups receiving each type of sentence (the similarities result from the randomization). The design ensures that sentence type is the only difference between the groups, which means that differences in outcomes following release result from the causal effect of the sentence type. The overall findings of these studies show that community service is no better than traditional custodial sentences in securing good outcomes for offenders.

However, while these studies are quite excellent in their design, they suffer from very small sample sizes, and this may account for the non-significant results. Hence we need more knowledge based on larger sample sizes before we can draw final conclusions on the effects of incarceration. Our study contributes to the existing literature on the effects of incarceration on post-prison public support dependency by exploiting the implementation of electronic monitoring (EM) in Denmark for specific types of offenders that would have been sent to jail prior to that implementation. We use full sample data, thereby avoiding the problems pertaining to small sample size that we observe in existing studies. As in a randomized experiment, our design facilitates exogenous variation in who gets which treatment (EM or the conventional custodial sentence). The instrument of randomization is the date of conviction, whereby this design relies on the existence of a historical control group. With this strategy, we find that serving with EM reduces public dependency rates among offenders following their release.

Why should we expect non-custodial sentences to matter?

One explicit purpose of imprisonment is to prevent recidivism by rehabilitating and restraining the offender. However, both scholars and practitioners seem to agree that incarceration also has less attractive consequences that the use of non-custodial sentences such as EM may help to avoid (Schwartz & Skolnick, 1962). The theoretical and empirical literature on the negative effects of incarceration identifies several explanations for the harmful effects of incarceration.

Stigmatization
One explanation emphasizes the stigmas related to imprisonment. A number of studies use experiments to demonstrate significant discrimination against job applicants with criminal records: By varying only the criminal history of otherwise

identical applicants, the studies demonstrate employers' reluctance to hire ex-offenders, even for positions that do not require the holders to have a clean record (Schwartz & Skolnick, 1962; Cohen & Nisbett, 1997; Pager 2003). These findings very well reflect Goffman's description of stigmas as "blemishes of individual character perceived as weak will, domineering or unnatural passions, treacherous and rigid beliefs, and dishonesty, these being inferred from a known record of, for example, mental disorder, imprisonment, addiction, alcoholism, homosexuality, unemployment, suicidal attempts, and radical political behavior" (Goffman, 1963: 3). Thus, in the absence of full knowledge of an individual – in this case, the applicant – the people in his or her social surroundings (e.g. potential employers) extrapolate from the knowledge obtained of the criminal record to unobserved individual characteristics. The image thus formed may or may not correctly describe the individual, but the studies demonstrate a common perception of ex-offenders that prolongs their informal punishment indefinitely.

While both offenders who serve custodial and non-custodial sentences are likely to suffer from stigmatization – as they both hold criminal records – we may well assume that people in their social surroundings make harsher judgment of the offenders who were incarcerated: The public is likely to perceive a prison term as a stronger marker of a bad personality than a non-custodial sentence. As a result offenders who serve non-custodial sentences may experience fewer stigmas than offenders who serve custodial sentences when their sentences are completed (Western et al, 2001).

Loss of capital

A second explanation emphasizes how incarceration affects human capital, by giving inmates fewer years at the ordinary labor market. This is likely to erode their job skills and restrict their possibilities of acquiring experience (Western et al. 2001; Waldfogel, 1994). This mechanism may not only apply to labor market experience, but could also affect an offender's opportunities for "investing" in other social relations, such as friendships and marriage, that could have promoted positive outcomes both at the labor market and in other domains (Hagan, 1993; Lopoo & Western, 2005). Thus, if ex-offenders have worse outcomes than others, this may result from their unstable affiliation with normal society, which prevents them from making continuous social investments. However, serving a non-custodial sentence will reduce offenders' period of absence from the society, which suggests that offenders who serve non-custodial sentences may have better outcomes after serving their sentences than offenders who serve custodial sentences.

It is possible to think of additional reasons why custodial sentences could be more harmful to the individuel than non-custodial sentences; a term in prison could accelerate the onset of mental illnesses, for example, and promote friendships with delinquent peers. Both these are processes that are likely to negatively affect post-release outcomes.

Negative effects of EM?

But while the literature presents several explanations for the effects of incarceration, we may also speculate as to whether EM is merely a conventional sentence without the prison element, or whether this type of non-custodial sentence involves other potentially useful or harmful elements that affect post-sentencing outcomes. For instance, whereas traditional custodial sentences facilitate a separation between offenders' criminal sphere and their other spheres (e.g. legal work and family life), EM will confuse these spheres, as the offender now serves his or her sentence while at the same time acting as an active member of a family and an active employee (Vitores & Doménech, 2003; Cassidy et al, 2005). In this way, the non-criminal sphere is no-longer unaffiliated with the offender's criminal life, and this may impair the use of the non-criminal sphere as a lever for desistance after the sentence has been served (see e.g. Sorensen & Kyvsgaard, 2009). EM may then impede desistance from crime among this group of offenders. In addition, one aim of imprisonment is to deter actual and potential future offenders from committing (further) crime both during and after incapacitation (e.g. Gorecki, 1979; Gibbs, 1988), and this deterrence is lacking from, or at least reduced with EM; and likewise one may argue that the general preventive effect from the threat of punishment will be lower with EM than traditional prison. As a result, offenders who are electronically monitored may not fully realize the implications of their wrongdoings, and consequently be less likely to desist from crime after completing the sentence, and we may see an increase in the general crime rate due to lower deterrence effects from EM.

Thus, while we may be able to think of several negative consequences of serving a prison sentence that result primarily from impairment of the offender's reputation and of his or her social and human capital, EM may also be far from ideal and may cause negative outcomes by affecting individual processes of desistance. In sum, we may expect negative outcomes for both offenders who are sent to prison and offenders who are electronically monitored; however, the common perception is that imprisonment leaves the offender worse off than EM. To identify the causal effect of EM on offenders' public dependency following their release, we exploit the implementation of the EM scheme in Denmark.

Electronic monitoring in Denmark

Denmark first introduced EM in May 2005. With the introduction of a new law, traffic offenders could serve sentences shorter than three months in their own homes, under intensive surveillance and control. This mainly involved EM and a strict organization of everyday life, especially with regard to activities outside the home. Offenders serving with EM also had to accept 1-3 unannounced weekly control visits that involved blood tests for alcohol and drug abuse (Law no. 367). To be allowed to serve his or her sentence this way, an offender had to have a permanent address (not be living in a shelter for the homeless, for example) and have a job, be participating in some form of active labor market program for the unemployed, or be enrolled in education. Unemployed offenders could fulfill this employment criterion by working at institutions appointed by the prison service. If the offender had cohabiting family members, these had to formally accept the EM. In addition, only offenders who had not previously committed any serious crime - defined as crime punishable by more than a fine - in a period of two years prior to the conviction, could serve this new type of sentence. Moreover, if the convicted offender failed to keep to certain conditions while serving the sentence, the sentence was converted into imprisonment. These conditions included avoiding crime, alcohol, and illegal drugs, sticking to the strict organization of everyday life laid down, and accepting the electronic monitoring. Last, offenders serving their sentences with EM were required to participate in a crime prevention program at the prison service premises.

In April 2006, the scheme was extended to include all offenders younger than 25 years of age at the time when the criminal act was committed, regardless of the crime (yet still with a maximum sentence of 3 months), and in June 2008 another change removed the age requirement (this last reform prohibited the use of EM for offenders convicted on charges of possession of weapons or explosives who were sentenced to less than 2 weeks imprisonment). Until recently, all offenders who received prison sentences of less than three months were eligible for this type of non-custodial sentence serving.[1]

Identification strategy

In Denmark, EM is not a sentence given by a judge; it is a way of serving a prison sentence. The judge sentences the offender to a prison sentence, and then the Department of Prison and Probation Service under the Ministry of Justice (DPPS) informs convicted offenders who fulfill the requirements listed above of the opportunity to serve their sentence at home with EM rather than in prison. If the offender wishes to serve at home, he or she then applies to the DPPS to do so, and the department makes the final decision on whether or not to grant the particular offender the right to serve at home with EM. Of the convicted offenders who apply for and are granted permission to serve this type of sentence, some have second

---

1 In 2010 the rules were changed so the maximum sentence length requirement is now set to 5 months. This reform lies outside our data window and is thus not considered.

thoughts, and in other cases the DPPS revokes the permission. In addition, some offenders begin the EM but violate the conditions and are then transferred to a conventional prison. Thus, not all offenders eligible to serve under EM apply for this type of sentence, and not all offenders who apply for this type of sentence actually end up serving at home. Obviously, this introduces selection issues that we must take into account in order to facilitate causal inference. An assessment of the EM scheme in Denmark conducted in 2009 shows that approximately 43 percent of the offenders who are offered the choice of serving their sentence under EM complete their sentences under this type of scheme (Sorensen & Kyvsgaard, 2009).

In effect, offenders who serve EM sentences represent a highly selected group, which means that we cannot assess the causal effect of this type of non-custodial sentence just by comparing the outcomes of offenders who serve with EM and offenders who serve conventional custodial sentences. These two groups are likely to differ on a range of observed and unobserved characteristics that would cause severe bias in the estimates (Gable & Gable, 2005). Instead, we exploit the implementation of the scheme where, from one day to the next, a group of offenders who would previously have faced traditional imprisonment now had the opportunity of serving their sentences at home under EM. Thus the reform represents a sharp discontinuity in offenders' chances of serving with EM that is uncorrelated with their individual observed and unobserved characteristics. Due to the complicated selection mechanisms explained above, we refrain from estimating the actual treatment effect on the treated (i.e. the effect of completing an EM sentence) as it is difficult to assess who would have been granted and completed EM before the scheme was introduced, and thus to find a suitable control group. Rather, we compare post-release public dependency rates for offenders sentenced before and after the reform, who fulfilled the formal criteria for being offered EM, and we thus estimate the average treatment effect. In effect, treatment is then defined as being sentenced after the reform. Under the assumption that the two groups are comparable on observed and unobserved characteristics, this strategy will provide us with a valid estimate of the causal effect of the reform.

Note however, that this assumption is violated if the introduction of EM changes judges' sentencing behavior. Lenient judges may sentence offenders to 3 months imprisonment instead of 4 to make them eligible for EM, and harder judges, who are less in favor of EM, may increase sentence lengths when expecting the offender to be offered to serve with EM. The same would apply if, for some other reasons, sentencing practices change over time. After the main analyses we conduct a sensitivity analysis to discuss such possible sources of bias.

Method
We calculate the treatment effect using two different approaches, the difference-

in-difference (DiD) estimator and difference-in-difference matching. The two estimators rely on different assumptions.

DiD estimators estimate the average treatment effect by comparing differences between treatment and control groups in post-release outcomes with differences between the same groups' pre-conviction outcomes,

$$(1) \quad \hat{\delta}_{DiD} = (Y_1^{D=1} - Y_0^{D=1}) - (Y_1^{D=0} - Y_0^{D=0})$$

where Y_0 denotes the pre-treatment outcome and Y_1 the post-treatment outcome. D indicates treatment status ($D=1$ are the treated, i.e. offenders sentenced after the particular reform, and $D=0$ are the controls, i.e. offenders sentenced before). To obtain a more precise DiD estimate, we add a range of controls to (1).

The DiD estimator exploits the panel structure of the data to eliminate all observed and unobserved time-in-variant differences between the two groups (treated and controls). This should produce unbiased estimates. However, if there are time-variant differences between the two groups, the DiD estimator yields biased results. In our setup, this could be the case if for instance differences in the two groups' public dependency history affect the observed change in their dependency rates from before to after the sentence.

To address possible concerns related to our model choice (the DiD), we also present results from DiD matching, a process that balances the two groups on observed pre-treatment characteristics, including public dependency history. In this model we base our treatment effect on groups that experienced the same time trends in dependency prior to the sentence. Assuming that the distribution of unobserved individual characteristics affecting selection into treatment and subsequent outcomes is similar across matched treated and controls, this DiD matching model reduces to simple propensity score matching, where the treated and the controls are balanced on pre-treatment outcome (Chabé-Ferret, 2010).

DiD matching estimates the average treatment effect by comparing the outcome of the treatment group to the outcome of the control group, weighted by some balancing score. The balancing score $P(X, Y_0)$ is predicted as each individual's propensity to receive treatment, given the individual's specific combination of covariates X and Y_0. Conditioning on $P(X, Y_0)$ then gives the DiD matching estimator,

(2) $\hat{\delta}_{DiD\ matching} = (\bar{Y}_1^{D=1}|P(X,Y_0)) - (\bar{Y}_1^{D=0}|P(X,Y_0))$

We report results from three different weights to test whether our results are sensitive to the choice of weight. These are 1:1 nearest neighbor (NN) matching, 1:10 NN matching, and kernel matching. We match with replacement and use only observations within the area of common support.

Data and variables

In Denmark, all residents have a unique social security number that identifies them in various transactions, e.g. visits to the doctor, enrolment in education, criminal charges and criminal convictions. All transactions are registered by the authorities concerned, and then collected by Statistics Denmark and linked into a yearly individual-level panel data set existing for all years from 1980 onwards. These records are our source of crime data and data on a range of background characteristics. We obtain information on public dependency from DREAM, an administrative database operated by the Ministry of Employment with weekly information on benefit receipts in Denmark. While the data from Statistics Denmark also contain information on unemployment and public dependency, the DREAM database contains the most recent information on individual-level benefit receipt in Denmark.

We exclude the first reform (Reform 1: May 24th 2005), which introduced EM as a serving type for traffic offenders in 2005, from the analyses. Only few individuals convicted within the first year following this reform actually ended up serving with EM. Also, the period was characterized by other changes in sanctions against traffic law offenders and results from this reform would then most likely be inconclusive due to the low observation numbers and biased due to the difficulties in finding suitable controls (cf. Jørgensen, 2011).

Considering the two remaining reforms, we use the registers to identify individuals sentenced to 3 months' imprisonment or less within a time window of +/- 365 days from the reform dates (Reform 2: April 21st 2006; Reform 3: July 1st 2008), and who are not sentenced to prison terms within 2 years prior to the relevant conviction. From this sample we delete a few cases where the offender is remanded in custody, who are imprisoned for previous offences when the conviction under observation is stated, who have unserved sentences where the unserved sentence and the present sentence together adds up to more than 3 months, or who commits new crimes while serving the present sentence. Last we delete cases where the offender does not carry through the sentence.

If D2 and D3 signify each of the reforms respectively, and D=0 for those convicted before a given reform (these are the controls) and D=1 for those convicted after it (these are the treated), we restrict offenders examined for D2 to offenders aged 25 or less at the time of the offence, and offenders examined for D3 to all offenders sentenced to less than 3 months' imprisonment except for those charged with possession of weapon or explosives and sentenced to less than 2 weeks' imprisonment.

Although we exclude the first reform, D1, from the analyses, we need to ensure that those who might be treated by this reform do not enter our data for the two later reforms, since this would compromise the comparison groups. Hence, we delete all traffic offenders from our data. Likewise, we need to ensure that those who might be treated by D2 do not enter our data for D3, and we hence delete all individuals below age 25 from D3. Our assessment of the effect of the second reform then relies only on offenders aged under 25, who were not convicted of traffic law offences, while our assessment of the effect of the third reform relies only on offenders aged above 25, who were not convicted of traffic law offences or on charges of possession of weapons or explosives who were sentenced to less than 2 weeks imprisonment.

Due to low numbers of women in data, we restrict our analyses to only include males. This leaves us with gross samples for the two reforms of 1,696 and 2,101 observations respectively. We exclude 133 and 22 observations respectively of people who served other types of non-custodial sentences (e.g. community service). Furthermore, we remove 187 and 170 observations respectively for people who disappeared from the records during our observation period due to death, migration, missing information in the registers or duplicate entries, and the like.

The last data selection step concerns the employment criterion for serving with EM. As mentioned previously, offenders may fulfill this criterion by working at firms appointed by the prison service. However, we cannot identify individuals in the control group who would have been offered and would have accepted such employment, and we therefore discard individuals in the treatment and control groups that appear in the unemployment register in the week of the start of the sentence. This reduces the samples to 1,055 (Reform 2) and 942 (Reform 3) individuals respectively. We show the numbers of treated and controls in each sample in Table 1, together with the number of "truly treated" (i.e. those who actually served with EM) in each treatment group. The first reform, D1, is included merely as reference.

Table 1: The reform samples. All those included are sentenced to no more than 3 months prison terms

Reform (D)	Reform date	Description	Control group	Treatment group	Truly treated
(1)	(May 24th 2005)	(Traffic offenders)	-	-	-
2	April 21st 2006	Below age 25, not traffic	474	581	332
3	July 1st 2008	Above age 25, not traffic*	472	470	297

* Except violators of the weapon law and the law on explosives sentenced to prison terms for less than 14 days.
Source: Own calculations based on data from Statistics Denmark.

Variables

Our outcome variable – individual level public support dependency, y_1 – is the average dependency rate for individuals during the first 52 weeks following the release date. More specifically, the individual level public support dependency rate is defined as the number of weeks an individual is dependent on public financial support other than publicly supported vacation or leave from employment, publicly supported parental leave, publicly supported education, public pensions or sick leave benefits, within a period of 52 weeks. The dependency rate then falls between 0 and 1 with 0 indicating no weeks of public support dependency and 1 indicating full 52 weeks of dependency. Note that since we do not have information on employment, we cannot know if individuals who do not receive any type of social benefits are self-supported through employment or though other sources (e.g. the income of a spouse). Table 2 shows the distribution of this variable in the samples, by treatment status. We observe that the dependency rate in the D2 sample is approximately .12 before treatment (y_0), indicating that on average, members of the sample were dependent on benefits for 12 percent of the year preceding their conviction. There are no significant differences between the treated and the controls prior to serving the sentence in this sample. After having served the sentence, however, there is a significant difference between the dependency rate of .13 for the treated compared to .17 for the controls. In the D3 sample the post-release dependency rate of the controls is approximately twice as high as the rate of the treated. These findings could reflect positive treatment effects in both the D2 and the D3 samples.

Table 2 also shows the distribution of the covariates included. They cover demographic variables, socioeconomic variables, labor market affiliation, and a description of criminal career characteristics, as well as information on sentence length. y_0 represents the pre-treatment outcome variable and measures the mean individual dependency rate during the 52 weeks preceding treatment. This is the variable used to calculate pre- and post-treatment differences in the DiD model and to balance the treatment and control group in the DiD matching analyses. ylag1, ylag26, and ylag52 are dummy variables that indicate dependency 1, 26, and 52 weeks before treatment. We use these only in the DiD matching to secure adequate balancing in the pre-treatment dependency slopes of the treatment and control groups. We include the remaining covariates in the DiD model and in the DiD matching to ensure that differences in post-release outcomes between the treated and controls do not arise from differences in observed characteristics. Overall, Table 2 shows that compared to the D3, the D2 sample has lower resources and a weaker affiliation to the labor market. They are more criminally active, and started their career at an earlier age.

Since the reforms used for our analyses are assumed to be exogenous, we do not expect any differences in the covariate distribution other than those that result from common statistical noise. However, as demonstrated in Table 2, there are differences between the treated and the controls. For D2 we find significant differences with regard to criminal careers and for D3 the differences center around labor market history. Both sets of differences are disturbing, as they signal systematic differences between treated and controls that contradict our assumptions of reform exogeneity. However, whether or not these differences will bias our results depends on the how they are dealt with in the models. Note also the significant difference in sentence length in D2 which could reflect judges' changed sentencing behavior mentioned previously. We will address this problem in a sensitivity analysis.

Table 2: Descriptive statistics

	D2		D3	
	Controls	Treated	Controls	Treated
Variable	Mean (sd.)	Mean (sd.)	Mean (sd.)	Mean (sd.)
Dependency rate (y_1)	.170 (.294)	.130 (.248) *	.224 (.350)	.121 (.254) ***
Lagged dependency rate (y_0)	.115 (.227)	.120 (.223)	.149 (.278)	.089 (.207) ***
Dependency rate 1 week before treatment (ylag1)	.002 (.046)	.000 (.000)	.000 (.000)	.002 (.046)
Dependency rate 26 weeks before treatment (ylag26)	.112 (.315)	.134 (.341)	.161 (.368)	.106 (.309) *

Dependency rate 52 weeks before treatment (ylag52)	.158 (.365)	.148 (.355)	.174 (.379)	.100 (.300) ***
Age	20.915 (2.165)	20.929 (2.212)	35.978 (8.469)	36.036 (8.613)
Single	.987 (.112)	.993 (.083)	.771 (.421)	.768 (.423)
Parent	.453 (.498)	.424 (.495)	.303 (.460)	.161 (.368) ***
Belongs to minority group	.207 (.405)	.217 (.412)	.180 (.385)	.164 (.371)
Out of labor force	.428 (.495)	.427 (.495)	.199 (.400)	.179 (.384)
In school	.169 (.375)	.141 (.348)	.015 (.121)	.015 (.121)
Highest education is elementary school	.911 (.284)	.916 (.278)	.555 (.497)	.549 (.498)
Gross income [a]	110.677 (94.840)	120.377 (101.719)	245.816 (187.748)	274.343 (222.040) *
Job type: Other [b]	.175 (.380)	.227 (.419) *	.210 (.408)	.251 (.434)
Job type: Crafts [b]	.215 (.411)	.215 (.411)	.216 (.412)	.181 (.385)
Job type: Service [b]	.084 (.278)	.117 (.322)	.097 (.297)	.079 (.270)
Job type: Knowledge [b]	.036 (.186)	.007 (.083) ***	.064 (.244)	.089 (.286)
Job type: No job [b]	.489 (.500)	.434 (.496)	.413 (.493)	.400 (.490)
Convicted for violence	.631 (.483)	.664 (.473)	.653 (.477)	.606 (.489)
Sentence length	40.544 (23.808)	44.855 (24.747) **	42.237 (22.325)	44.694 (23.787)
Suspended sentence length	16.346 (45.302)	8.057 (37.024) **	6.729 (31.151)	2.509 (14.312) **
Age at criminal debut	17.923 (2.047)	17.728 (1.983)	23.423 (8.441)	22.658 (8.363)
Total # of convictions	3.059 (3.270)	3.596 (3.381) **	7.150 (7.259)	7.543 (7.774)
Days since last crime committed	1,961.542 (2,864.148)	1,341.126 (2,351.692) ***	2,643.996 (4,210.558)	2,520.498 (4,072.336)
Total # of incarcerations [c]	2.578 (3.220)	2.552 (3.224)	4.246 (6.412)	4.383 (6.441)
Total days incarcerated [c]	12.211 (40.970)	15.862 (44.910)	57.640 (129.553)	56.604 (118.948)
N	474	581	472	470

* p < .05; ** p < .01; *** p < .001
[a] Gross income is reported in DKK 1,000 (2009 prices)
[b] Job type refers to the position held in November the year before treatment
[c] Including arrests
Source: Own calculations based on data from Statistics Denmark

Results

This section presents the results from the DiD and the DiD matching analyses. However, first we show descriptive evidence of the differences between our treated and controls in D2 and D3 in public support dependency rates before and after the reform. Figures 1 and 2 depict the weekly dependency rates for +/- 52 weeks from release/start of sentence (the time served is excluded) for our two samples. As explained, all offender groups have no dependency in the week of the sanction's initiation. The two figures show marked differences in post-release outcomes. For D2, these post-release differences are clear despite the lack of pre-conviction differences. This indicates that serving a sentence with EM due to the D2 reform affects dependency for groups who experienced the same trends in labor market affiliation prior to serving their sentences. Figure 2 shows the dependency "effect" of the third reform (D3). The figure shows (significant) differences in both pre- and post-release dependency rates. This suggests that the third reform is not strictly exogenous, and this finding emphasizes the need for proper statistical models to account for possible selection bias.

Figure 1: Average weekly dependency rates before and after time served, D2

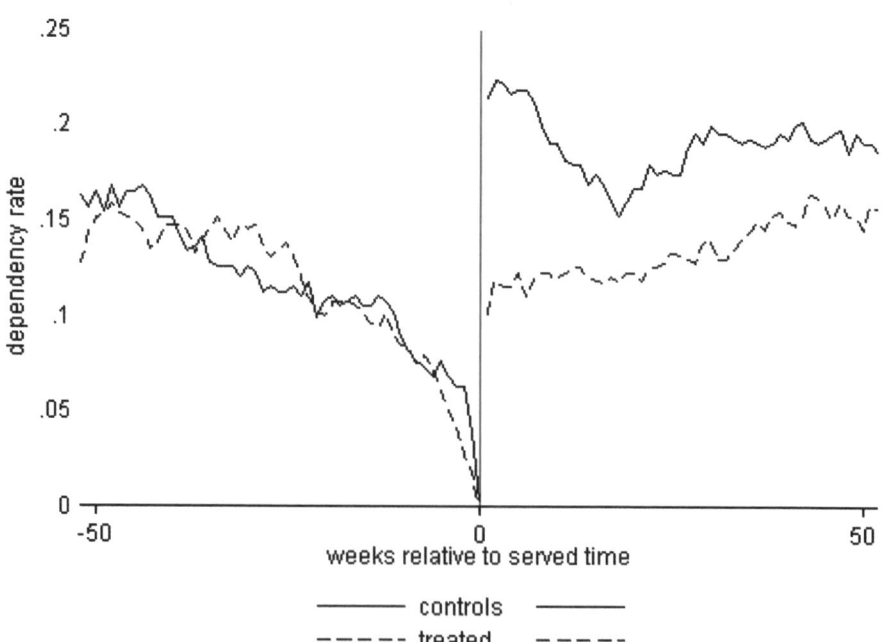

Source: Own calculations based on data from Statistics Denmark

Figure 2: Average weekly dependency rates before and after time served, D3

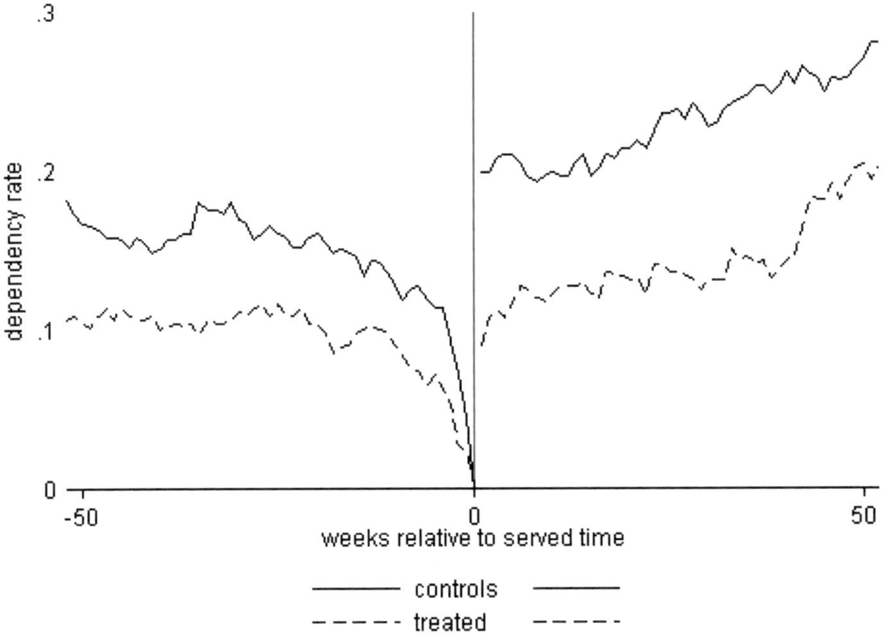

[Figure: Line graph showing dependency rate (y-axis, 0 to .3) versus weeks relative to served time (x-axis, -50 to 50), with two lines: controls (solid) and treated (dashed). Both lines drop sharply to 0 at week 0, then rise after, with controls remaining higher than treated.]

Source: Own calculations based on data from Statistics Denmark

Results from DiD and DiD matching analyses

Table 3 shows results from the different models: the simple DiD, the covariate adjusted DiD, and DiD matching models with three different weighting algorithms. The DiD matching results are particularly important for the evaluation of the effect of the third reform.

As seen, we find a large degree of consistency within samples across model types, with minor exceptions. All models except the 1:1 nearest neighbor matching find significant negative effects of the second reform. The effect sizes vary only little across models, indicating that offenders who serve with EM experience between 4.5 and 5.7 percent less dependency during the first 52 weeks following their release. The effect is nontrivial, as 5 percent of a year equals 18 days. Also, all models show a significant negative effect of Reform 3, albeit the estimate from the 1:1 nearest neighbor matching is only marginally significant. The effects are larger, numerically, than the effects of Reform 2: however, they vary more across model types, as the DiD matching models produce larger estimates than the two DiD models. We get the largest estimate of -.069 in the kernel matching, corresponding to an effect of 7 percent or 25 days of public support dependency.

The differences in results from the two model types are interesting, and may suggest that the different time trends in the public dependency histories of the treated and the controls depicted in Figure 3 reduces the validity of the DiD estimates, as the assumption of common time trends is then not fulfilled. However, the balancing procedure of the DiD matching ensures that we only compare offenders with similar pre-treatment time trends, and this should then make the DiD matching estimates more valid. Figure A1 in the appendix shows great similarities in pre-treatment time trends in the dependency rates of the two samples after the matching, just like Tables A1-A2 in the appendix shows no significant differences between the covariate distributions in the matched samples.

Table 3: Causal effect estimates (standard errors in parentheses)

Estimator	D2	D3
Simple DiD	-.045 (.016) **	-.043 (.017) **
Covariate adjusted DiD	-.053 (.017) **	-.045 (.018) *
1:1 NN matching	-.031 (.028)	-.063 (.035) †
1:10 NN matching	-.053 (.022) *	-.062 (.025) *
Kernel matching	-.057 (.019) **	-.069 (.023) **

† $p < .10$; * $p < .05$; ** $p < .01$; *** $p < .001$
Source: Own calculations based on data from Statistics Denmark

Sensitivity analysis

As described earlier, we assume that the reform introducing EM is exogenous to offender characteristics. However, this assumption is violated if judges change their behavior either as a result of the reform, or for other reasons. As explained earlier, lenient judges may for instance sentence offenders to 3 months imprisonment instead of 4 to make them eligible for EM, and harder judges, who are less in favor of EM, may increase sentence lengths when expecting the offender to be offered to serve with EM. Judges' sentencing behavior may also change for other reasons, due to other alternations of the punitive system or due to changing rhetorics about punishment in society. Both situations will either decrease or increase lengths of sentences after the reform, and we would mismatch treated and controls in the DiD matching models and pick a wrong control group for the DiD estimates. As a consequence the results presented in Table 3 would be biased.

We investigate this by first comparing the distribution of sentence lengths before and after each reform for the relevant groups. This is a check to see whether more offenders get short or long sentences across the reforms and, in particular, if more offenders get sentences just over or under the threshold of 92 days. Recall that this threshold determines whether offenders are eligible for EM or not.

From Table 2 we already know that sentence lengths seem to increase slightly after both reforms. For the second reform, D2, the increase amounts to approximately 4 days – the increase is significant – and for the third reform, D3, it is 2 days. However, these changes only reflect changed sentence lengths for offenders who are sentenced to less than 92 days, and are therefore not indicative of changes across this threshold. Also, such differences in means only reflect part of a potential change in the distribution and may disguise changes in specific areas of the distribution, rather than for all offenders. Thus, to investigate whether the length of sentences change across the reforms, we compare density plots of sentence lengths for those convicted +/- 365 days of each reform date. We focus on sentences that release prison terms lasting between 1 and 150 days.

Figures 3 to 4 show these densities – in each figure does the dashed line ("after") correspond to sentence length densities of the treatment group, and the solid line ("before") correspond to densities of the control group. The vertical line shows the threshold of 92 days. As can be seen, there are only minor differences between these two groups. Figure 3 shows how fewer offenders in the D2 treatment group get shorter sentences and more get longer sentences. This indicates a general "push to the right" for offenders affected by the second reform, and may reflect a changed sentencing behavior among judges, either as a result of the reform or for other reasons. In figure 4 it is difficult to identify differences between the two groups, and it seems that sentence lengths are quite stable across the third reform, D3.

Figure 3: Density plot of sentence length, D2

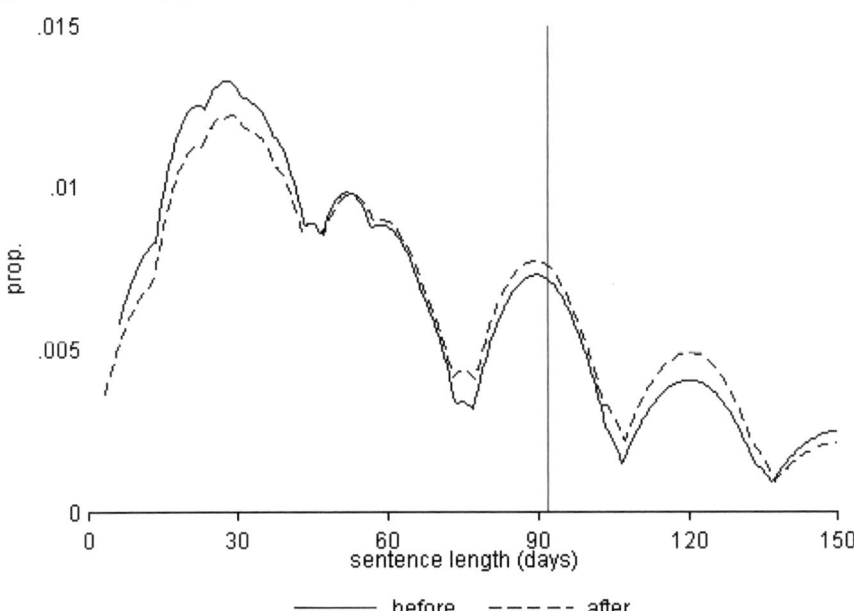

Source: Own calculations based on data from Statistics Denmark

Figure 4: Density plot of sentence length, D3

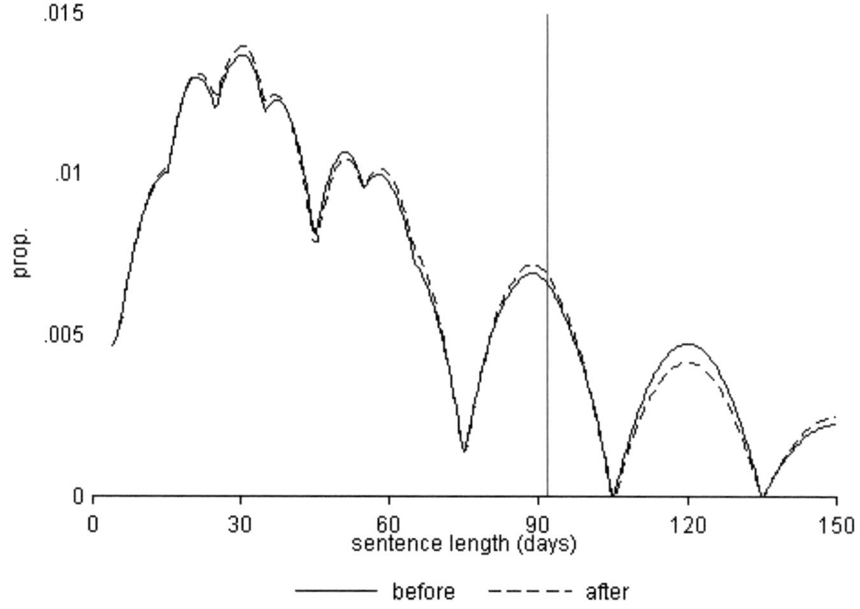

——— before   ----- after

Source: Own calculations based on data from Statistics Denmark

However, if we focus more narrowly on offenders who get sentences of just over or under 92 days (the EM threshold), there are no indications that judges have changed behavior across the reforms to secure more or fewer EM servers (as described above). We do not see any indications that more offenders receiving less than 92 days is paralleled by less offenders receiving more than 92 days, or vice versa (results not shown). Thus we have no reasons to suspect bias in our results arising from judges' explicit reactions to the implementation of EM.

Nevertheless, the change in sentence length across reforms – observed for especially D2 – may still bias our results. If they reflect an increase in sentence length that is uncorrelated with offender characteristics, we would have mismatched treated and controls in our matching models, because we match on sentence length. In that case we overestimate the treatment effect, as treated are then matched with worse controls, as defined by their sentence length.

Consequently, in this section we conduct sensitivity analyses, where we add the average difference in sentence length before and after the reform in question, to the sentence of individuals in the control group (that is we artificially push the control group to the right). We then rerun the analyses presented in Table 3, and present results that are adjusted for this potential change in judges' sentencing behavior. Table 4 shows the results of this analysis, and we see that the overall conclusions do not differ from those of Table 3. Still, two points needs noticing. First, the estimates from the D2 sample are slightly smaller than those of Table 3, and second, the estimates from the D3 sample are slightly larger than those of Table 3.

Table 4: Estimates from pseudo tests with controls' sentence length adjusted for possible change in sentencing behavior (standard errors in parentheses)

Estimator	D2	D3
Simple DiD	-.036 (.016) *	-.043 (.017) *
Covariate adjusted DiD	-.045 (.017) **	-.044 (.018) *
1:1 NN matching	-.040 (.030)	-.074 (.034) *
1:10 NN matching	-.055 (.019) **	-.070 (.023) **
Kernel matching	-.047 (.019) *	-.071 (.025) **

* $p < .05$; ** $p < .01$; *** $p < .001$
Source: Own calculations based on data from Statistics Denmark

If the increase in sentence length is uncorrelated with observed offender characteristics, we would then have overestimated the treatment effect in D2, yet underestimated it in D3. Importantly, both sets of results (presented in Tables 3 and 4) points in the same direction and allows us to conclude that offenders are better off serving with EM, rather than in prison.

Last, it is worth considering whether changes in the business cycle may drive our results. Importantly, both reforms (D2 and D3) happen at or after the onset of the global economic crisis, and in Denmark, unemployment increased annually from the onset of this crisis. This suggests that if anything, our treated individuals in both samples finish their sentences at times where the labor market is worse off than when the controls finish their sentences. This would then cause a downward bias in our results, which suggest that in times of a stable economic situation, our treatment effect would have been even bigger.

However, we test this empirically by normalizing the dependency rates in our two samples by the dependency rates (for the relevant years) in a sample of non-convicted men in comparable age groups. Table 5 shows the results, and as seen and as was expected, results based on the normalized dependency rates are even larger than our original results, presented in Table 3. This suggests that, provided that we used an adequate (i.e. sufficiently comparable) group for normalizing the dependency rates, our original estimates are slightly downward biased. Overall, this then does not jeopardize our original results.

Table 5: Estimates based on normalized dependency rates (standard errors in parentheses)

Estimator	D2	D3
Simple DiD	-.058 (.016) ***	-.057 (.018) **
Covariate adjusted DiD	-.068 (.017) ***	-.061 (.019) **
1:1 NN matching	-.057 (.032)	-.078 (.030) *
1:10 NN matching	-.067 (.021) **	-.088 (.019) ***
Kernel matching	-.067 (.023) **	-.081 (.021) ***

* p < .05; ** p < .01; *** p < .001
Source: Own calculations based on data from Statistics Denmark

Discussion and conclusion

In this paper we show how serving a sentence with EM rather than actually going to prison affects the post-release dependency rates of offenders. Our results clearly indicate that type of sentence does matter. The first reform that introduced EM as a type of sentence serving for traffic offenders in Denmark has not been analyzed in the present paper due to a low number of observations and other challenges, and we therefore note that our results are applicable only to offenders sentenced to no more than 3 months and not for traffic offences.

However, the second and third reforms, which resulted in more people serving their sentences with EM, do seem to have made a difference, as both offenders below and above 25 years of age benefitted from serving this type of non-custodial sentence compared to if they had instead served a traditional custodial sentence. We see this from the consistently significant estimates across models specified in different ways. All models clearly indicate that offenders who served their sentences with EM exhibited lower benefit dependency rates after release, compared to offenders who went to prison. This then suggests that more efforts should be made to organize and implement the use of non-custodial sentences.

That being said, our outcome measure does have some limitations that are important to mention. As described above, we determine the measure as average weekly social benefit dependency. However, weeks without benefits may be either weeks in employment or weeks with other types of self-support. Such self-support may include being supported by a spouse, waiting to become eligible for benefits, or engaging in dubious activities, including criminal activities. Thus, we cannot necessarily interpret the absence of benefits in any given week positively, as such absence may reflect either socially useful or non-beneficial activities. This suggests that we should also look at other outcome measures, such as recidivism, to assess the full effect of the EM scheme. Unfortunately, due to data limitations, this was not possible in the current analysis, yet according to a recent report conducted by the Ministry of Justise, those treated by D2 have 15 percent lower recidivism rates than the controls within a two-year follow-up period – and 24 percent lower recidivism rates to serious crimes (Jørgensen, 2011). Qualitative interviews (Jørgensen, 2011) suggest that these significantly lower recidivism rates are fostered by the strict organization of everyday life that is associated with serving time with EM.

In addition, it is important to mention that our conclusions relate to the specific group of offenders included in our analyses. If policy makers decide to extend the EM sentence to other offender groups, the effect may be different.

Appendix

Figure A1: Average weekly dependency rates before and after time served, D3 matched sample (kernel)

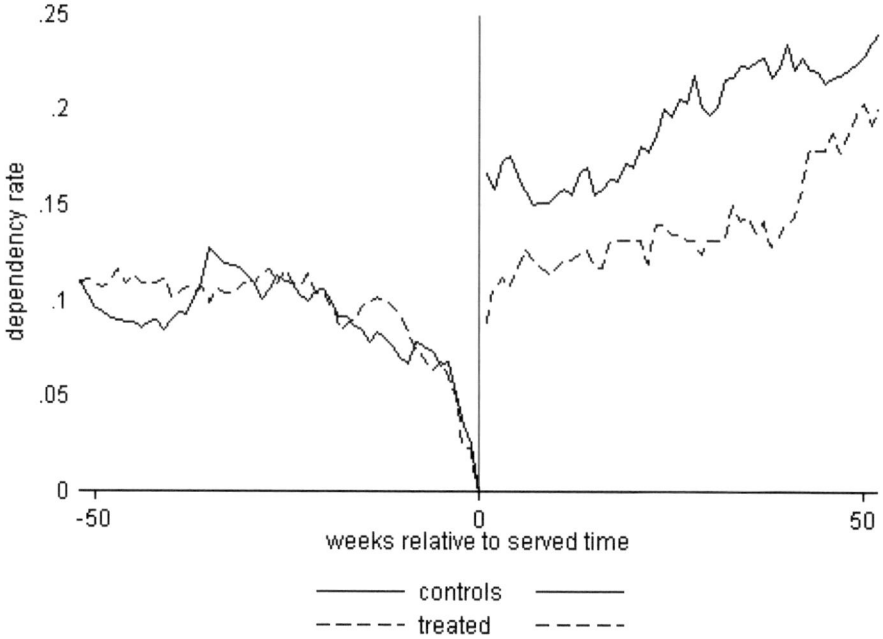

Source: Own calculations based on data from Statistics Denmark

Table A1: Covariate distribution in matched samples from 1:1 NN matching

1:1 NN	D2		D3	
Variable	Controls	Treated	Controls	Treated
Lagged dependency (y_0)	.122	.110	.097	.092
Dependency 52 weeks before treatment (ylag52)	.152	.168	.112	.100
Dependency 26 weeks before treatment (ylag26)	.134	.110	.117	.109
Dependency 1 week before treatment (ylag1)	.000	.000	.000	.000
Age	20.942	20.765	35.923	36.651
Single	.993	.996	.782	.760
Parent	.421	.441	.167	.187
Belongs to minority group	.217	.192	.164	.120
Out of labor force	.426	.444	.182	.182
In school	.144	.187	.016	.016
Highest education is elementary school	.913	.941	.551	.540
Gross income [a]	119.700	110.120	261.480	267.460
Job type: Crafts [b]	.217	.210	.189	.191
Job type: Service [b]	.112	.147	.082	.067
Job type: knowledge [b]	.007	.005	.078	.118
Job type: No job [b]	.435	.407	.396	.376
Convicted for violence	.661	.657	.611	.647
Sentence length	44.014	44.510	44.489	45.560
Suspended sentence length	7.817	10.911	2.620	2.467
Age at criminal debut	17.704	17.650	22.569	22.648
Total # of convictions	3.600	3.753	7.484	8.093
Days since last crime committed	1,316.400	1,294.000	2,448.600	2,333.600
Total # of incarcerations [c]	2.592	2.629	4.340	5.056
Total days incarcerated [c]	15.218	17.149	58.024	73.040
N	459	563	458	450
Pseudo R-squared	.014		.014	
LR Chi squared	20.64		17.18	

* $p < .05$; ** $p < .01$; *** $p < .001$
[a] Gross income is reported in DKK 1,000 (2009 prices)
[b] Job type refers to the position held in November the year before treatment
[c] Including arrests
Source: Own calculations based on data from Statistics Denmark

Table A2: Covariate distribution in matched samples from 1:10 NN matching

1:10 NN	D2		D3	
Variable	Controls	Treated	Controls	Treated
Lagged dependency (y_0)	.122	.129	.097	.092
Dependency 52 weeks before treatment (ylag52)	.152	.167	.112	.106
Dependency 26 weeks before treatment (ylag26)	.134	.135	.117	.109
Dependency 1 week before treatment (ylag1)	.000	.000	.000	.000
Age	20.942	20.917	35.923	36.235
Single	.993	.993	.782	.767
Parent	.421	.432	.167	.170
Belongs to minority group	.217	.214	.164	.158
Out of labor force	.426	.454	.182	.201
In school	.144	.163	.016	.011
Highest education is elementary school	.913	.911	.551	.540
Gross income [a]	119.700	118.280	261.480	257.390
Job type: Crafts [b]	.217	.213	.189	.174
Job type: Service [b]	.112	.114	.082	.088
Job type: knowledge [b]	.007	.009	.078	.095
Job type: No job [b]	.435	.437	.396	.406
Convicted for violence	.661	.666	.611	.625
Sentence length	44.014	44.748	44.489	43.519
Suspended sentence length	7.817	9.069	2.620	2.462
Age at criminal debut	17.704	17.723	22.569	22.751
Total # of convictions	3.600	3.587	7.484	7.604
Days since last crime committed	1,316.400	1,286.300	2,448.600	2,481.800
Total # of incarcerations [c]	2.592	2.593	4.340	4.493
Total days incarcerated [c]	15.218	15.312	58.024	56.366
N	469	563	458	450
Pseudo R-squared	.004		.004	
LR Chi squared	5.87		4.33	

* $p < .05$; ** $p < .01$; *** $p < .001$
[a] Gross income is reported in DKK 1,000 (2009 prices)
[b] Job type refers to the position held in November the year before treatment
[c] Including arrests
Source: Own calculations based on data from Statistics Denmark

Table A3: Covariate distribution in matched samples from kernel matching

Kernel	D2		D3	
Variable	Controls	Treated	Controls	Treated
Lagged dependency (y_0)	.122	.134	.097	.092
Dependency 52 weeks before treatment (ylag52)	.152	.168	.112	.103
Dependency 26 weeks before treatment (ylag26)	.134	.145	.117	.111
Dependency 1 week before treatment (ylag1)	.000	.000	.000	.000
Age	20.942	20.897	35.923	36.190
Single	.993	.993	.782	.777
Parent	.421	.433	.167	.170
Belongs to minority group	.217	.220	.164	.144
Out of labor force	.426	.445	.182	.201
In school	.144	.149	.016	.014
Highest education is elementary school	.913	.917	.551	.552
Gross income [a]	119.700	118.330	261.480	258.610
Job type: Crafts [b]	.217	.208	.189	.178
Job type: Service [b]	.112	.114	.082	.080
Job type: knowledge [b]	.007	.009	.078	.097
Job type: No job [b]	.435	.446	.396	.399
Convicted for: Violence	.661	.662	.611	.611
Sentence length	44.014	44.612	44.489	43.637
Suspended sentence length	7.817	9.346	2.620	2.558
Age at criminal debut	17.704	17.719	22.569	22.718
Total # of convictions	3.600	3.579	7.484	7.448
Days since last crime committed	1,316.400	1,292.700	2,448.600	2,442.900
Total # of incarcerations [c]	2.592	2.591	4.340	4.468
Total days incarcerated [c]	15.218	15.185	58.024	59.677
N	469	563	458	450
Pseudo R-squared	.004		.004	
LR Chi squared	5.59		4.99	

* $p < .05$; ** $p < .01$; *** $p < .001$
[a] Gross income is reported in 1,000 DKK (2009 prices)
[b] Job type refers to the position held in November the year before treatment
[c] Including arrests
Source: Own calculations based on data from Statistics Denmark

References

Bushway, Shawn D. & Paternoster, Raymond (2009): The Impact of Prison on Crime. In Raphael, Steven & Stoll, Michael A. (eds.): *Do Prisons Make us Safer? The Benefits and Costs of the Prison Boom*. Russel Sage Foundation.

Cassidy, Davnet, Harper, Gemma & Brown, Sarah (2005): Understanding electronic monitoring of juveniles on bail or remand to local authority accommodation. *Home Office Online Report*, 21/05.

Chabé-Ferret, Sylvain (2010): To Control or Not to Control: Bias of Simple Matching vs Difference-In-Difference Matching in a Dynamic Framework. *Unpublished Paper* found at http://www.cerdi.org/uploads/sfCmsNews/html/2782/Chabe_Ferret_26_nov_2010.pdf.

Cohen, Dov & Nisbett, Richard E. (1997): Field experiments Examining the Culture of Honor: The Role of Institutions in Perpetuating Norms about Violence. *Personality and Social Psychology Bulletin*, 23(11): 1188-1199.

Gable, Ralph Kirkland & Gable, Robert S. (2005): Electronic Monitoring: Positive Intervention Strategies. *Federal Probation*, 69(1): 21-25.

Gibbs, Jack P. (1988): Toward Theories about Criminal Justice. *Journal of Contemporary Criminal Justice*, 4: 20-36.

Goffman, Ervin (1963): *Stigma: Notes on the management of spoiled identity*. Englewood Cliffs, NJ: Prentice Hall.

Gorecki, J. (1979): *A theory of criminal justices*. New York: Columbia University Press.

Hagan, John (1993): The social embeddedness of crime and unemployment. *Criminology*, 31(4): 465-491.

Jorgensen, Tanja T. (2011): *Afsoning i hjemmet. En effektevaluering af fodlænkeordningen*. Justitsministeriets Forskningskontor. Found at http://www.justitsministeriet.dk/fileadmin/downloads/Forskning_og_dokumentation/Rapporter/Afsoning_i_hjemmet_-_En_effektevaluering_af_fodlaenkeordningen.pdf

Justice Policy Institute Report (2000): The Punishing Decade.

Killias, Martin & Villetaz, Patrice (2008): The effects of custodial vs. non-custodial sanctions on reoffending: Lessons from a systematic review. *Psicothema*, 20(1): 29-34.

Killias, Martin, Gilliéron, Gwladys, Villard, Francoise & Poglia, Clara (2010): How damaging is imprisonment in the long-term? A controlled experiment comparing long-term effects of community service and short custodial sentences on re-offending and social integration. *Journal of Experimental Criminology*, 6: 115-130.

Law no. 367, issued May 24th 2005, found at https://www.retsinformation.dk/Forms/R0710.aspx?id=2076 on September 16th 2011.

Lehmann, Christian (2008): Straffen skærpes, kriminaliteten er den samme. *Information*, 11/7-2008.

Lopoo; Leonard M. & Western, Bruce (2005): Incarceration and the Formation and Stability of Marital Unions. *Journal of Marriage and Family*, 67(3): 721-734.

Pager, Devah (2003): The mark of a criminal record. *American Journal of Sociology*, 108: 937-975.

Raphael, Steven & Stoll, Michael A. (2009): Introduction. In Raphael, Steven & Stoll, Michael A. (eds.): *Do Prisons Make us Safer? The Benefits and Costs of the Prison Boom*. Russel Sage Foundation.

Renzema, Marc & May-Wilson, Evan (2005): Can electronic monitoring reduce crime for moderate to high-risk offenders? *Journal of Experimental Criminology*, 1: 215-237.

Schwartz, Richard D. & Skolnick, Jerome H. (1962): Two Studies of Legal Stigma. *Social Problems*, 10(2): 133-142.

Sorensen, Dave & Kyvsgaard, Britta (2009): *Afsoning i hjemmet: En forløbsanalyse vedrørende fodlænkeordningen*. Justitsministeriets Forskningsenhed. Found at http://www.justitsministeriet.dk/fileadmin/downloads/Forskning_og_dokumentation/Rapport_om_forlaenkeforloebet.pdf.

Villettaz, Patrice, Killias, Martin & Zoder, Isabel (2006): *The Effects of Custodial vs. Non-Custodial Sentences on re-Offending: A Systematic Review of the State of Knowledge*. Campbell Systematic Reviews, 2006: 13.

Vitores, Anna & Doménech, Miquel (2003): From Inhabiting to Haunting: New Ways of Social Control. In Hård, Mikael, Lösch, Andreas & Verdicchio, Dirk (eds.): *Transforming Spaces. The Topological Turn in Technology studies.* Found at http://ifs.tu-darmstadt.de/gradkoll/Publikationen/transformingspaces.html.

Waldfogel, Joel (1994): The Effect of Criminal Conviction on Income and Trust "Reposed in the Workmen". *Journal of Human Resources*, 29(1): 62-81.

Western, Bruce, Kling, Jeffrey R., & Weiman, David F. (2001): The labor market consequences of incarceration. *Crime and Delinquency*, 47: 410-427.